20TH CENTURY MEDIA

1900–20

SOUND AND LIGHT

20TH CENTURY MEDIA – 1900–20
was produced by

David West 👫 **Children's Books**
7 Princeton Court
55 Felsham Road
London SW15 1AZ

Picture Research: Carrie Haines
Designer: Rob Shone
Editor: James Pickering

First published in Great Britain in 2002 by
Heinemann Library, Halley Court, Jordan Hill,
Oxford OX2 8EJ, a division of Reed Educational and
Professional Publishing Limited.

OXFORD MELBOURNE AUCKLAND
JOHANNESBURG BLANTYRE GABORONE
IBADAN PORTSMOUTH (NH) USA CHICAGO

06 05 04 03 02
10 9 8 7 6 5 4 3 2 1

ISBN 0 431 15250 0 (HB)
ISBN 0 431 15264 0 (PB)

British Library Cataloguing in Publication Data

Parker, Steve, 1952-
20th century media 1900 - 1920: sound and light
1. Sound - Equipment and supplies - History -
Juvenile literature 2. Light - Juvenile literature
I. Title II. Twentieth-century media 1900-1920
621.3'893'09041

Printed and bound in Italy

PHOTO CREDITS :
Abbreviations: t-top, m-middle, b-bottom, r-right,
l-left.

Cover m, 5t, 24t, 25tr, 25bl - Lebrecht Collection.
Cover bl, 6l, 8-9, 9t & br, 14tr, 15ml & b, 17tr, 20bl,
22-23, 23tr, 26tl & mr, 28tl & 29tl - AKG. Cover br,
3, 4 both, 4-5, 6tr, 7r, 8l, 9mr, 10 both, 11br, 12l, 13bl
& m, 14bl, 15tl, 16bl, 18l, 18-19 both, 19 both, 21tl,
23br, 24b, 27tr, 28br, 29tr - Mary Evans Picture
Library. 4b, 4-5, 12-13, 26bm, 28-29 - Dover Books.
5r, 6-7, 11bl, 12r, 16-17b, 21mr, 29br - Hulton
Archive. 7br - The Art Archive/Ocean Memorabilia
Collection. 11tr, 20m & t, 22 both - The Kobal
Collection. 13tr - The Culture Archive. 16tr & 25bm -
The Art Archive/Dagli Orti. 17br - Courtesy of the
Clark Collection of the Smithsonian Institution & Dr
Frank R. Millikan. 27bl - Science & Society.

*The dates in brackets after a person's name
give the years that he or she lived.*

*An explanation of difficult words can be
found in the glossary on page 30.*

20TH CENTURY MEDIA

1900-20
SOUND AND LIGHT

Steve Parker

Heinemann
LIBRARY

CONTENTS

THE MASS MEDIA
5

TITANIC SINKS!
6

READ ALL ABOUT IT
8

THE PRESS BARONS
10

SEARCH FOR THE TRUTH
12

NEWS ON THE WIRE
14

THE WIRELESS BEGINS
16

ON THE RADIO
18

THE MOVING IMAGE
20

SILENT MOVIES
22

STORING SOUND
24

PHOTOS GROW UP
26

AT WAR!
28

GLOSSARY & TIMELINE
30

INDEX
32

NEWSPAPERS
Before radio and television, newspapers were the main medium for finding out about the latest events.

INTRUSION
Even a century ago, media were intruding or 'poking' into people's private lives.

LA VIE PARISIENNE   LENDEMAIN DE GALAS   Dessin de André Hellé

LE CAUCHEMAR PRÉSIDENTIEL

THURSDAY, DECEMBER

Daily Tribune

with incredulity and disgust.

TIME

THE MASS MEDIA

What are the big news stories today? Perhaps a new singer has topped the music charts. A movie star has bought a new car. And thousands of people are fleeing from an erupting volcano. We find out what is happening in the world around us through the media. We are often entertained by the media too. The media spread, pass on or communicate news, knowledge, information and opinions. Mass media reach millions.

Today's mass media include television, radio, newspapers, magazines, photographs and other images, music and movies, and of course, computers linked to the Internet. A century ago, around 1900, the media were very different. There was no television or Internet. Even so, the business of mass media was huge and powerful. Bosses raced to find better, faster media technologies, to keep them one step ahead of their rivals.

"HIS MASTER'S VOICE"

STORED SOUNDS
We now have tapes, vinyl, CDs, DVDs, MP3s and various other forms of music and recorded sound. But this medium was only just beginning in the 1900s.

5

TELEGRAMS
At the start of the 20th century, telephones were rare in ordinary homes. Urgent messages were sent along telegraph wires, printed out as words on paper at the local office, and delivered by messengers.

NEW MEDIUM
The 'moving pictures' of the cinema were only a few years old in 1900. People were quick to develop this new medium, both for news stories and information, and for entertainment.

TITANIC SINKS!

It was one of the worst disasters the world had ever known. On the night of 14–15 April 1912, the giant ocean liner *Titanic* was on its first voyage, from Southampton in England to New York, USA. But the ship hit an iceberg in the north-west Atlantic Ocean, near the Grand Banks of Newfoundland. Within just three hours she had sunk, with the loss of some 1,500 lives.

SHOCK AND HORROR

Some ships of the time, including *Titanic*, had 'wireless telegraphy' – basic radio equipment. This could send and receive messages using the dots and dashes of Morse code. *Titanic* sent out distress signals after it hit the iceberg. One ship was nearby, the *Californian*, but its radio operator was off duty. So help was delayed by many hours, which greatly increased the death toll. As the news was relayed by radio to Europe and North America, the media began to carry stories of the great disaster.

LA PERTE DU PLUS GRAND PAQUEBOT DU MONDE
Le "Titanic" a sombré après être entré en collision avec un iceberg

Concours du Supplément du PETIT JOURNAL N° 4

BERG'S EYE VIEW
There were no photographs of the terrible collision between ship and iceberg. But news illustrators and artists soon created views of the event, using photos of Titanic and plenty of imagination.

EMERGING TRAGEDY
As relatives queued for news of passengers and crew, at the offices of Titanic's shipping company, the White Star Line, journalists began to reveal important new information. The liner was supposed to be unsinkable, owing to its 16 separate watertight compartments. So it only had enough lifeboats for about half of those on board.

THE RISING TOLL

There were no radio broadcasts in 1912, so newspapers were the main news medium. They brought out extra editions, several each day. Even experienced reporters struggled to find words to express the horror. Information filtered through over hours and days, and the death toll rose – 1,000, 1,100, 1,200 …

POSITIVE RESULTS

Several newspapers led campaigns to ensure that a shipwreck on the scale of *Titanic* could not happen again. Long-haul plane journeys had not begun, and ships were the main form of ocean travel. The campaigns led to reforms such as lifeboat space for everyone on board, lifeboat drills, a full-time radio watch while at sea, patrols for icebergs and other hazards, and a global agreement called the International Convention of Safety of Life at Sea.

Ship radio rooms had to be manned at all times.

LESSONS TO LEARN

Investigations into the disaster were carried out by the shipping authorities, and also by reporters keen to make sure that there were no cover-ups. It seemed that several factors together had contributed to the great loss of life, which was finally put at about 1,510. *Titanic* was going too quickly in foggy conditions, its over-confident designers had not provided enough lifeboats, and help was too slow to arrive.

REMEMBERED IN MANY WAYS

The story of Titanic *quickly spread around the world. Like any great but tragic event, it became the subject of stories, songs, plays and movies. This is the Hebrew version of one such song.*

READ ALL ABOUT IT

There are several main kinds, or groups, of media. Broadcast media include radio and television, and use radio waves sent out from transmitters. These began after 1920. In 1900 the main kinds of media were print – newspapers, magazines, journals and periodicals.

PRINTING PRESS
Presses were huge and noisy, needed constant care, and occasionally broke down. Teams of engineers and mechanics stood by at all times.

INTO PRINT

Newspapers raced each other at every stage. Each one tried to get its reporters to the scene of an event first. The reporter's story and any photographs were sent by messengers, or along telegraph wires, to the main newspaper office. Layout staff designed the pages, while compositors worked by hand or at large machines, arranging tiny blocks of metal which carried the letters, or type, for the words.

LAST LINK
Newspaper production began with on-the-spot reporters. The final links in the long process were street vendors.

EAST END MURDER POLICE HUNT
12 O'CLOCK EDITION

OFFSET LITHOGRAPHY

In 1900 there were several methods of printing. In letterpress the image area (area to be printed) is raised in height above non-print areas. In lithography (litho) both are level, but only the image area has a surface texture that attracts the grease-based ink. In offset litho the ink is transferred, or offset, to a second or blanket surface, to save wear on the original litho surface. It was invented in 1904 by American printer Ira W. Rubel.

3 Image areas on print cylinder accept ink, water-damp non-image areas reject it

5 Image prints from blanket cylinder on to paper

2 Ink rollers carry grease-based ink on to print cylinder

1 Water rollers dampen non-image areas on print cylinder

4 Inked image is transferred, or offset, on to blanket cylinder

FIVE INTO ONE

In hand typesetting, tiny metal blocks, each with a letter or number, were stored in cases. Workers picked out the correct ones to arrange into words and lines. One automatic composing machine could do the work five times faster.

AUTO-TYPE

Hand typesetting (left) was slow and laborious. The process was automated from the 1880s by companies such as Monotype and Linotype. A compositor 'composed' the words. He sat at a keyboard and typed in the story. The machine selected and arranged the small metal blocks carrying letters, numbers, spaces and symbols.

Keyboards were used to set up or 'compose' the type.

THE PRESSES ROLL

In 1900 the words and pictures were in the form of raised parts on a metal surface. In the printing press, ink was put on the raised areas and then pressed on to sheets of paper passing by. The sheets were cut into pages, collated (put in the correct order), loaded on to horse-drawn carts or the newly-invented motorized trucks, and rushed out for sale in shops and on street corners.

ONE STEP AHEAD

It was a breathless business with several versions, or editions, of a paper through the day. Each had the very latest news. A breakdown or delay meant rival newspapers would be on the streets first. Inventors worked on new technology to speed up the process. One such advance was the method of printing called offset lithography (left).

KEY ROOM

Every day, every newspaper needed every word tapped in by keyboard. This 1902 composing room served just one English city paper, the Sheffield Daily Telegraph.

THE PRESS BARONS

Read the papers – all the news and views from around the world! Not really. We can only find out a tiny amount of everything that happens. Newspaper people have already chosen which information we receive, and how it should affect us.

POWER AND INFLUENCE

In the early 20th century, newspapers were the main medium for current events. A paper's editor controlled day-to-day production, chose which stories went in – and which ones made the front page. The paper's owner also had huge influence on the kinds of events covered, and how they were reported. Read one paper and a certain politician was doing well. Read another and he was a failure. Editors and owners shaped the news, and so had enormous power over the public.

HEARST (1863–1951)
Hearst was a keen supporter of the rights of ordinary people – when it suited him.

PAPERS TO POLITICS
Hearst built up a vast newspaper empire. He and Pulitzer competed by publishing stories in a wild, sensational style known as yellow journalism. Hearst also tried to become US President (1904) and governor of New York (1908, left), but failed.

STORY OF A NEWSPAPER TYCOON

Citizen Kane (1941), directed by and starring Orson Welles, is viewed as one of the all-time great movies. It tells the story of newspaper boss Charles Foster Kane, whose career was loosely based on the life of William Randolph Hearst. The exciting events involve media, business, politics, love, fame and fortune. They show how a media tycoon might use his enormous power to make himself even more successful, by reporting favourably on his own business affairs and political views. When Kane is told that his papers describe trivial events, which are not real news, he replies: 'Make the headlines big enough, and they become news!'

Charles Kane (actor Orson Welles) makes a political speech.

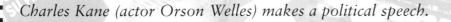

PULITZER (1847–1911)

Joseph Pulitzer began his career as a journalist in St Louis. He rose to newspaper owner and added sports, cartoons and fashion to 'hard news'. He was also active in politics. His name lives on in the yearly Pulitzer Prize for American journalism.

THE TYCOONS

Many men rose to power through their papers. Joseph Pulitzer's *New York World* helped to develop the modern style of newspaper. His fierce rival was William Randolph Hearst, who renamed his *New York Morning Journal* as the *American* (1901). At one stage Hearst controlled 36 papers and owned magazines, movie companies and, later, radio stations. In Britain, Alfred Harmsworth (later Lord Northcliffe) had a similar empire and in 1903 founded the *Daily Mirror*.

FASTER NEWS

Edward W. Scripps (1854–1926) founded the United Press Association in 1907. It used telegraphs and the newer telephones to carry news faster. News or press services gathered the information, then sold it as stories to the papers.

WORKING LATE
Editors had to be available at all times, to assess the latest big stories and receive hot news over the telephone.

SEARCH FOR THE TRUTH

The media report on important events which interest the public. But some people want certain events kept secret. Investigating them can be risky, even dangerous. Media reporters may get mixed up in scandal, corruption, crime and cover-up.

FINDING OUT
Journalists used many methods to get the facts. Sometimes they were accused of crimes themselves, such as trespass or theft of documents.

THE MUCKRAKERS

Investigative journalists or crime reporters try to find out what really goes on behind the scenes, rather than simply accept what the public is told. They work in similar ways to the police or private detectives. They try to expose criminals and uncover wrong-doings. In the early 1900s, a group of US journalists began to write articles in magazines such as *McClure's* and *Collier's*. They described illegal examples of slave labour, racial discrimination, crooked deals by business leaders, and bribes taken by politicians. They were called the Muckrakers, a name started by US President Theodore Roosevelt in about 1906. The trend of investigative journalism soon spread to Europe and other regions.

THE VERDICT

BE SURE AND ASK FOR THE SUPPLEMENT.

ALFRED HENRY LEWIS, Editor.

NEW YORK, (FOR WEEK ENDING) MARCH 13, 1899.

VOL. I.   NO. 13.   MIRS.

PRICE, TEN CENTS. 20 PAGES.

ROOSEVELT'S IDEA OF REORGANIZATION.

POWERFUL PICTURE
Before Roosevelt became US President, he was Governor of New York. Some people disliked his methods of reform, but others approved. This cartoon shows him grinding up politicians to get his own way.

12

EVENTS ABROAD

Another trend from the 1900s was to report more news from around the world. This became quicker and easier, because reports and photographs could be sent long distance along wires, rather than by messenger or postal service. People learned more about distant lands – including their wars, famines and disasters.

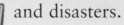

STORIES IN CARTOONS

Comic strips began as newspaper or magazine 'extras' to help sales. From about 1900 they gained fame in their own right. They dealt with all kinds of issues from amusing pets and home life to world politics. *The Yellow Kid* (1890s) was followed by George McManus' *Newlyweds* (1904) and *Bringing Up Father* (1913), and George Herriman's *Krazy Kat* (1911).

Papers that carried R.F. Outcault's Yellow Kid, *became known as 'yellow papers' (see page 10).*

FOREIGN NEWS, 1904
An Italian newspaper shows an artist's view of battlefield horrors almost half a world away in the Russian-Japanese War.

CAUSING HARM?
A Danish cartoon of 1908 wonders if stories containing violence cause real-life harm. If so, should traditional fairy tales like Little Red Riding Hood be banned?

BAD INFLUENCE

Some parts of the media were accused of harmful effects on the public, especially children. Stories and cartoon strips often showed weapons and fighting. Did this encourage violence among readers? The arguments continue today.

13

NEWS ON THE WIRE

From ancient times, words and pictures were sent from one place to another in physical form – usually on pieces of paper. The telegraph changed this. It sent words along wires as electrical signals. The telephone went further. It carried speech, also in an instant.

THE 'CABLE'

Because telegraph signals went along cables (wires), the messages themselves became known as 'cables'. This telegram or cable marks a great moment in history. It was sent by the Wright Brothers to their father, telling him about their very first aeroplane flights, in December 1903.

THE WESTERN UNION
23,000 OFFICES IN AMERICA.
ROBERT C. CLOWRY, P

RECEIVED at   Via Nor

1.76 c KA CS 33 Paid.
Kitty Hawk N C Dec 17
Bishop M Wright   7 Hawthorne St

Success four flights thursday morning   all against twenty one mile wind started from Level with engine power alone average speed through air thirty one miles longest 57 seconds inform Press home ~~cheys~~ Christmas .

Grevelle Wright   525P

TELEGRAPH EXCHANGE

Telegraph operators connected their machines into the fast-growing network and controlled them by hand.

PICTURES BY WIRE

The telegraph sent words and numbers as codes of electrical signals. In 1904, Johann Elster made a device, the photoelectric cell, which could detect shades of black and white in a picture and produce a similar pattern of electrical signals. Later that year in Germany, the first pictures were sent along telegraph wires. This was a great advance for the newspapers.

Sending pictures by telegraph, in a 1912 book.

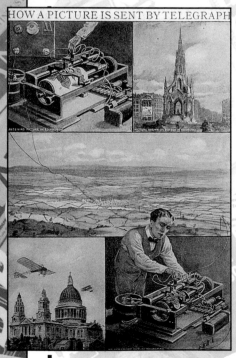

HOW A PICTURE IS SENT BY TELEGRAPH

OLD AND NEW

The telegraph had been around since the 1830s, when US artist-inventor Samuel Morse devised his code of dots (short electrical pulses) and dashes (long ones) for letters and numbers. By 1900, automatic machines read Morse code as holes in paper tape at 400 words per minute. In 1874 Emile Baudot invented the multiplex system, where six messages could be sent along the same wire at once, by a very fast time-sharing process. Baudot's system became popular in Europe.

'BELL HERE ...'

Alexander Graham Bell saw his invention become part of everyday life during the early 1900s. He was guest of honour and first to speak at the opening of many long-distance lines.

THE TELEPHONE

The telephone was invented by Scottish-American speech expert Alexander Graham Bell in 1876, in Boston, USA. It was seen as a rival to the telegraph. But the telephone carried speech, while the telegraph sent written words, and later, pictures. Both systems had their uses and so they grew side by side for many years.

MOUTHPIECE

Sound waves in
Diaphragm vibrates
Carbon granules
Electric current out
EARPIECE
Sound waves out
Diaphragm
Electro-magnets
Electric current in

AT THE SPEED OF LIGHT

Also in the 1900s, the telephone was spreading rapidly. Both telegraph and telephone signals are electrical, and electricity travels at the speed of light, which can go around the Earth seven times in one second. This allowed news reports and other information to be sent long distances almost instantly, rather than by messengers. Journalists could read their stories over the phone to head office, where they were typed and ready to print in a few minutes. But the growth of telegraphs and telephones meant that streets were soon a maze of tall poles carrying hundreds and thousands of wires, belonging to different companies, and each going to individual houses and offices.

15

A WEB OF WIRE
Telegraphs and telephones enjoyed booming business as poles and wires spread through towns and across the countryside.

CENTRAL EXCHANGE
In the 1910s cities became choked with masts, poles, wires and cables. This diagram from about 1920 in Germany shows how the wires could be put safely out of sight in underground tunnels or pipes. They joined up in a central building, the telephone exchange.

THE WIRELESS BEGINS

During the 1890s Guglielmo Marconi developed an entirely new form of communication. It used invisible waves passing through the air. Unlike the telegraph and telephone, no wires linked the sender and receiver. It became known as 'wireless'.

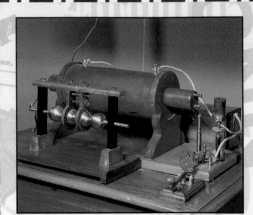

Early Marconi transmitter.

MARCONI

Guglielmo Marconi (1874–1937) made his first radio equipment in 1895 at his family home near Bologna, Italy. He tested the early versions in the attic. Then he moved into the garden, so he could send the signals farther.

RADIO WAVES

The invisible waves were called Hertzian waves, after the scientist who had first produced them in 1888, Heinrich Hertz. We now call them radio waves. They are similar in nature to light waves and travel at the same speed. Marconi called them radio-telegraphy waves. He used them to carry messages, by sending them in on-off pulses, as in the Morse code signals of the telegraph.

TELEGRAPH BY RADIO

Early radio equipment did not send messages for voices or music. Neither did it receive them – general radio broadcasts would not happen for several years. Marconi's first 'wireless' systems copied the Morse code method of the telegraph. Marconi's Wireless Telegraph Company was set up in 1900. Some of the earliest radio users were ships at sea, especially for sending emergency messages. Unlike telegraph users on land, they could not be linked by wires!

ONE OF MARCONI'S EARLIEST EXPERIMENTS

ACROSS THE ATLANTIC

By 1898 Marconi, based in London, had set up a network of radio masts around England. He reported on a yacht race in the Irish Sea by radio-telegraphy, from a boat to nearby Kingstown, and the news was sent on by telephone to the papers. In 1901 he sent radio signals across the Atlantic. This exciting new way of sending information across the globe, in an instant, itself became world news.

16

THE CAT'S WHISKERS

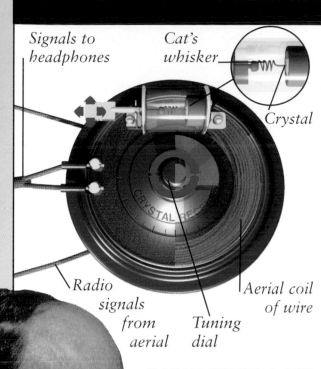

Signals to headphones

Cat's whisker

Crystal

Radio signals from aerial

Tuning dial

Aerial coil of wire

EARLY CRYSTAL SET

In 1900, German physicist Karl Braun adapted his earlier studies of crystals, and used them as electrical devices called diodes. These were important parts of radio receivers and led to the simple receiver called the crystal set. It picked up radio waves in a long wire, the aerial. The set included another wire, the 'cat's whisker', which was adjusted to tune into different programmes. These early radio receivers had no batteries, electricity supply or loudspeaker. They used the energy in the radio waves themselves, to power very small headphones. So only one or two people could listen.

KARL BRAUN
Radio pioneers Marconi and Braun shared a Nobel Prize in 1909.

LEE DE FOREST
In 1907, US scientist De Forest invented the triode valve. This boosted or amplified electrical signals, and was a vital advance in making radio equipment much more powerful.

METHOD TO MEDIUM

Many scientists worked to make radio equipment smaller, lighter and more powerful. At first, radio was a specialized method of sending messages by Morse code, including news reports and then pictures. But in 1906, radio operators on ships in the North Atlantic were startled to hear, not beeps of code, but a human voice coming out of their radio sets. Radio was developing into a medium of its own, for news and entertainment – as shown on the next page.

RADIO SPEAKS
Reginald Fessenden sent out the first radio signals to carry the sound of a voice (his own) and music (Handel's), on 24 December 1906.

ON THE RADIO

In the early 1900s, radio was a very new technology. The equipment was big, expensive, difficult to operate and not very reliable. Messages were sent in blips of Morse code.

SPECIAL USES

At first, radio was limited to special uses such as the police, emergency services, armed forces, ships and early aeroplanes. Quickly news organizations and the newspapers took it up, since it greatly speeded the reporting of events. Gradually more ordinary people became involved in radio, and started to form clubs and groups. But it was still an enthusiast's hobby for the public. Most messages were sent by Morse code or a similar coding system.

Le Petit Journal

SUPPLÉMENT ILLUSTRÉ
DIMANCHE 14 AOUT 1910

ARRESTATION DU DOCTEUR CRIPPEN ET DE MISS LE NEVE
SUR LE PONT DU «MONTROSE»

NO ESCAPE
Dr Crippen was arrested in the Atlantic on the liner Montrose. *A radio message said he was trying to escape after murdering his wife.*

RADIO 'FIRSTS'

The first radio messages to carry speech and music were sent in 1906 (see page 17). This meant more people could understand them, especially the news announcements. They could also enjoy listening to music, since recordings of music on discs were still very rare and expensive. One of the earliest big-news events to spread quickly by radio was the death of Britain's King Edward VII in 1910. Also in 1910, Dr Crippen (above) became the first criminal to be caught by radio.

In the early 1920s, an English family listens to a concert from Holland, 300 kilometres away.

BANNED, THEN UNBANNED

In 1912, new international laws said all large ships should have radios, for use in an emergency. This did not stop the sinking of *Titanic* in the same year. However radio messages did help to lessen the tragedy, even though assistance came late.

When World War One began in 1914, the use of radio was banned in many countries. The armed forces did not want public broadcasts to interfere with their own secret 'wireless' messages. After the war finished in 1918, the bans were gradually lifted. By about 1920, radio was set to expand hugely. Early public broadcasting stations were set up by Marconi near Chelmsford, England, and at East Pittsburgh, USA.

NEW SHOPS
By 1920 radio was establishing itself as a new, exciting medium. An unfamiliar type of shop sprung up in almost every town.

'IS THAT THE GARAGE?'
By the 1910s–20s radios were small enough to carry in cars, to call for help in the event of a breakdown. Such in-car transmitter-receivers were an early form of today's mobile phones.

NEW TECHNOLOGY

After Marconi's early work on radio, many other scientists improved the 'wireless'. Reginald Fessenden developed better oscillators which made an electric current reverse to and fro very quickly in a transmitter aerial, to produce radio waves. Fessenden also devised a better type of receiver. In 1918, another US inventor, Edwin Armstrong, made it much easier to tune into different broadcasts with his super-heterodyne receiver. A new family pastime was to cluster around the crackling 'wireless set'.

WIRELESS IN WARTIME
Marconi helped to improve radio sets during World War One. These showed the importance of radio in battle. Before this, messages were sent by riders on horse, motorcycle or cycle, by plane or even by pigeon!

THE MOVING IMAGE

The first moving picture show was in Paris in 1895. The films, or movies, had been made by the Lumière brothers, who also invented the equipment. By 1900, the cinema had caught on in a big way, for both news and entertainment.

ALMOST MOVING PICTURES

From 1872 English photographer Eadweard Muybridge experimented with many cameras in a row. Each took a photo as the animal went past.

RUN FOR YOUR LIFE

Auguste and Louis Lumière made more than 1,600 films. In one of the first, a train comes towards the screen. Some viewers, unsure if it was real, ran away in terror!

THE BIG SCREEN

Before about 1900, for art and entertainment, people went to live performances at theatres and concert halls. The Lumières changed this. They were inspired by a one-viewer-only moving picture machine called the Kinetoscope, invented by Thomas Edison. In 1894 the brothers began work on the Cinématographe. It was a movie camera, to take many still photos per second, and a projector to show them on a screen for many viewers.

THE LUMIERES

The Lumières made their first films in Lyon, France, in 1895. Within ten years, cinema had become a major new medium and art form.

CINÉMATOGRAPHE LUMIÈRE

HA-HA!
The Lumières'
Teasing the Gardener *was the first
film comedy. A boy stands on the hose, the
gardener looks into it, the boy steps off ... squirt!*

IMMEDIATE HIT

The Cinématographe and its big-screen pictures
were an instant sensation. Within a year or two,
'motion picture theatres' or cinemas were
growing in many cities. Early films were mostly
scenes from real life, perhaps changed slightly to
make them funny or sad. Conjuror Georges
Méliès began to use special effects, as in *A Trip
to the Moon* (1902). By stopping the camera,
adding or taking away an object, and starting
again, magical effects were obtained.

BIRTH OF A BUSINESS

Once a live performance was captured
on film, it could be shown almost
anywhere, time and time again. The
amazing growth of cinema as a new
medium greatly worried actors, singers,
musicians and other performers. They
thought it might put them out of work. In
some cases, this was true,
especially in variety theatre.
But other performers found
blossoming careers and
greater fame in the new
movie business.

THE KINETOSCOPE
Edison's 'peep-hole'
Kinetoscope showed 15-
second films of daily
life. Edison himself
thought that films
would not appeal to
the public. He did
not get involved
in movies until
others showed
they were
successful.

*Kinetograph
(camera for
the Kinetoscope).*

THE CINE CAMERA

The cine camera
exposes film by
allowing light on to a
strip of photographic
celluloid. It forms a
series of still photos
in fast succession,
called frames. When
these are shown on a
screen, the eye blurs
them together to give
the impression of
continuous motion.

Unexposed film
Gate (hole)
Shutter
Lenses

*The revolving shutter allows light through
a gate on to the film (1), as the
claw behind moves back.
The shutter cuts off light,
the claw pokes into the
hole in the film strip (2)
and moves it down
one frame (3). The
turning shutter again
lets light through to
the next frame (4).*

1
2
3

Exposed film 4

SILENT MOVIES

Books which simply describe people's daily lives would not be popular. The first movies were like such books. But soon film-makers began to write exciting plots with action-packed scenes in exotic places, and weave them together to make gripping new adventure stories.

THE GREAT TRAIN ROBBERY
This 1903 film used many new techniques, such as cameras that moved along, different locations and cutting from one part of the story to another.

NOT REAL LIFE

Early films were usually recorded in one scene by one camera in one place. However, some film-makers wanted to use the new medium of cinema in fresh ways. Stop the camera, move it to a new location, start it again, and you could 'cut' boring parts such as people walking along, and keep the action going. Many such methods were developed from about 1900. Also different styles of movies appeared – historical epic, comedy, crime drama and thriller. Cinemas boomed, especially in France and the USA.

THE KEYSTONE KOPS
From 1912, Irish-Canadian Mack Sennett made Keystone Kops movies. He developed slapstick humour, chaotic accidents and madcap chases.

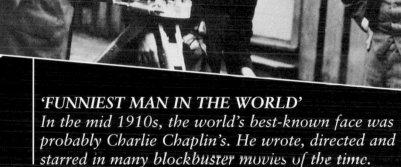

SMALL BEGINNINGS

At first, short movies were shown in variety theatres, in between live acts. From about 1905, films moved into small cinemas, often converted from high-street stores. In the USA these 'nickelodeons' held up to 200 people. They showed about six 10-minute films including a comedy, an adventure and a newsreel.

MAJOR ART

Film-makers wanted to produce longer, more ambitious movies. One of the greatest was D.W. Griffiths. In 1915, his three-hour epic *The Birth of a Nation* told the story of the American Civil War and its aftermath. Film stars such as Rudolph Valentino, Mary Pickford, Fatty Arbuckle, Theda Bara and Clara Bow became household names.

'FUNNIEST MAN IN THE WORLD'
In the mid 1910s, the world's best-known face was probably Charlie Chaplin's. He wrote, directed and starred in many blockbuster movies of the time.

NEWS AT THE CINEMA

Cinema was used to inform as well as to entertain. Many people could not read newspapers, and there was little radio and no television. So films showing recent events, called newsreels, were a major medium for spreading the news. In 1896, French businessman Charles Pathé set up a film company that grew to be the world's biggest until about 1915. From 1908, his Pathé-Journal newsreels showed current events from around the world.

INTRODUCING THE "TANKS" TO LONDONERS
THE BATTLE OF THE ANCRE—AT THE SCALA THEATRE

Audiences watch news of battles from World War One.

STORING SOUND

In 1901, German-born US engineer Emile Berliner founded the Victor Talking Machine Company. It made a device that recorded or stored sounds in the form of a long spiral groove in a flat rotating disc. Berliner had been working on his invention, which he called the gramophone, since 1887. His Victor Company began the mass-production sound recording industry.

EDISON'S TALKING MACHINE
Edison predicted that the main use for his phonograph would be as a 'talking machine'. It would record spoken letters and reports, for writing or typing later.

THE PHONOGRAPH

Edison's phonograph and Berliner's gramophone used similar technology to gather sound waves, turn them into vibrations and store these as a wavy groove. In the phonograph the groove went round and round a cylinder. Early versions made the groove in metal foil. In the 1880s, the groove was cut into hard wax. For a time, cylinders produced better sound quality than discs. But they soon wore out, and making copies was very difficult. By the 1910s Edison began to abandon cylinders in favour of discs.

An Edison phonograph and cylinders (below).

RIVAL SYSTEMS

Berliner's great rival in sound recording was Thomas Edison, who had invented a similar system earlier, in 1877 (left). Berliner developed the gramophone to improve the sound quality, and also to make thousands of copies from one original recorded disc, the 'master'. These advances gave the gramophone the edge over the phonograph. People began to buy gramophones and discs in large numbers, and the business thrived.

24

BERLINER AT NUMBER ONE
Berliner used a plastic-like substance called shellac, produced by certain insects, for his discs. Each disc was 30.5 centimetres (12 inches) across and stored up to five minutes of recorded sounds.

A NEW MEDIUM

For many people, recorded sound was still a novelty. They were amazed to hear speech and music coming from a machine rather than from live performers. But, like cinema, sound recording soon became art and entertainment – a medium in its own right. Actors, singers and musicians made recordings for Berliner's discs. Among these early voices were established concert performers such as Enrico Caruso, John McCormack and Fyodor Chaliapin. By 1920, in the USA, Bell Telephone Laboratories were developing electrical versions of the system. A microphone picked up the sounds, and a loudspeaker played them back.

THE GRAMOPHONE

The gramophone was mechanical, needing no electricity. A funnel-shaped horn gathered sound waves, which vibrated a flexible drum-like sheet, the diaphragm. This fed the vibrations to a needle-shaped stylus, which cut a wavy groove in a master disc. Playback was the same process in reverse. A handle or clockwork motor turned the disc.

Sounds out
Diaphragm vibrates
Sound horn
Stylus
Grooves
Disc
Drive wheel

FIRST BIG STAR
Italian opera singer Enrico Caruso made his first records in 1902. He became the world's first star of recorded sound.

DREAMS OF LONG AGO
COMPOSED BY
ENRICO CARUSO
Sung by CARUSO on VICTOR RECORD No 88376

OTHER SONGS BY CARUSO
With English and Italian Words
THE SONG OF SPITE (Canzona a Dispietto)
OLDEN TIMES (Tiempo Antico)
THE FORSAKEN WINDOW (Fenesta Abbanduneta)

ENGLISH VERSION by EARL CARROLL

LEO FEIST NEW YORK

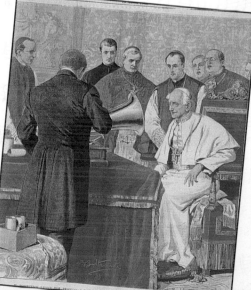

THE POPE ON RECORD
Many speeches were made into recordings, here by the Pope in 1903 – there was no radio.

PHOTOS GROW UP

Photography became an important medium in the mid-19th century. Most photographs were visual information about real life, from portraits of presidents and kings, to views of the countryside, to news reports of tragedies or the terrible scenes of a battle.

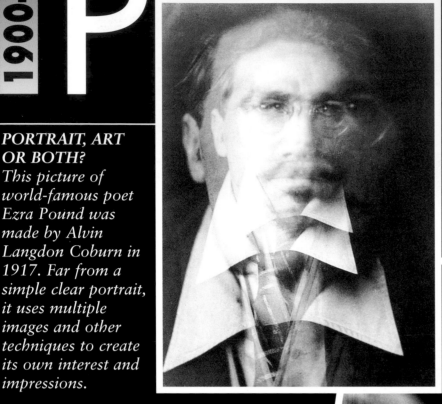

PORTRAIT, ART OR BOTH?

This picture of world-famous poet Ezra Pound was made by Alvin Langdon Coburn in 1917. Far from a simple clear portrait, it uses multiple images and other techniques to create its own interest and impressions.

A NEW FORM OF ART

However, from about 1890, experts argued that the medium of photography might not always record real life. It could be an art form. Painters and sculptors produced works of art from imagination. Why not photographers? Photos could be valued for their own beauty and fascination, and for the feelings they aroused in viewers. Photo-Secession began in New York, USA in 1902, to help make photography an accepted medium for art.

PHOTO-REPORTAGE

Lewis Hines used the medium of photography in a serious way, for social change. His images of child workers show no obvious horror, but aroused great sadness.

CAMERAS OF THE TIME

The year 1900 saw the launch of 'mass production' Kodak Brownie cameras. Kodak aimed to make photography available to all, not just to experts.

BEAUTY, NOT TRUTH

Leaders of Photo-Secession were Alfred Stieglitz, with Alvin Langdon Coburn, Edward Steichen, Gertrude Käsebier and Clarence White. They believed photographs could simply be beautiful, rather than useful or true to life. They might be made by combining images, altering light levels, making parts blurred or hazy, and other techniques. The group was a major force in establishing photography as an art form. From 1903 it produced the journal *Camera Work*. In France, Eugène Atget developed similar opinions after taking many different pictures of real-life scenes.

RECORDING REAL LIFE

Photo-journalists continued to record scenes and events for newspapers and magazines. In the USA, Lewis Hines took pictures of child workers in factories. The tragic plight of young people working long hours for almost no pay aroused strong feelings and helped to change society.

NO PRIVACY

As cameras became smaller and easier to use, photos could be taken almost anywhere. People of interest to the media were not only 'snapped' in their public lives, but also in private moments. Some rich and famous people began to complain about media intrusion and lack of privacy.

Invasion of private life, 1908.

OLD FAMILIAR FLOWERS

This autochrome photograph dates from 1919.

AUTOCHROME PHOTOGRAPHY

Colour photography was made practical in 1907 by the Lumière autochrome process. Tinted chemicals made from potato starch filtered out different colours of light. The resulting images had many bright yet delicate hues and a slightly patchy, spotty quality. (Modern colour film dates from the 1930s.)

Orange grains — Violet grains — Green grains

1 Glass plate (or flexible film) coated with adhesive

2 Dyed but transparent grains of starch added as coloured filters

3 Varnish and light-sensitive layer added to plate

AT WAR!

The media become extremely important during a great event. World War One (1914–18) was the biggest and bloodiest event of all. People wanted the latest information about who was doing what and why. The news media had powers to change public views and shape national opinion.

CARTOON FUN
A cartoon makes feared enemies into ridiculous figures of fun. Here the British national character 'John Bull' is irritated by enemy 'wasps' in the Boer or South African War (1899–1902).

28

A TIME OF CONFLICT

The news media should try to report truthfully, keeping events in proportion so that minor stories do not become huge headlines. But there is so much news every day, it cannot fit into one newspaper. Someone must 'choose the news' and select the reports that people will read.

What about a country at war? Selecting news stories becomes more difficult. Government and armed forces get involved. There are secrets to keep. Should media power help the war effort and whip up national support? Reports can contain true facts, but also make the enemy seem worse and more evil than it is.

RUSSIA IN REVOLT
The Russian Revolution of 1917 saw the ruling Tsar and his family overthrown. This picture shows ordinary working people taking power.

THURSDAY, DECEMBER 31, 1902

SUPPORT THE WAR
A 1917 US poster shows how buying wisely could stop the threat of enemy invasion.

HELP STOP THIS

W.S.S.

BUY W.S.S.
& KEEP HIM OUT of AMERICA

FILMING UNDER FIRE
War photographers risk injury or death to supply news images. This camera is protected by an armoured shield.

DIFFERENT NEWS

World War One involved all European nations, and affected almost every country on Earth. More than eight million soldiers died. But the newspapers of countries on different sides might have been reporting different conflicts. Each had huge headlines for battles won, but reported losses less fully. Readers on every side were told that they were fighting a just cause. They cannot all have been right. Only years later, when the full facts are known, can a balanced view emerge. If that ever happens.

'OUTRAGE: INNOCENTS SLAUGHTERED AT SEA'

In May 1915 the huge British passenger liner *Lusitania* was sunk in the West Atlantic, by a German submarine torpedo. Germany justified the action, saying the ship carried war weapons and equipment. About 1,200 of the 1,900 people on board died. The event made huge headlines in the USA, where the media emphasized that 128 Americans were among those lost. This helped to swing US public opinion in favour of joining the war against Germany, which the USA did in 1917.

The New York Herald *reports the* Lusitania *tragedy.*

THE NEW YORK HERALD

THE LUSITANIA IS SUNK; 1,000 PROBABLY ARE LOST

GERMANS TORPEDO THE GIANT STEAMSHIP AND SHE FOUNDERS EIGHT MILES FROM IRISH COAST

RESCUE VESSELS SPEED TO THE SCENE TO PICK UP SURVIVORS ONLY 601 ARE ACCOUNTED

GLOSSARY

BROADCAST MEDIA News and information sent out to many people – that is, broadcast – usually in the form of radio (electromagnetic) waves, as radio and TV programmes.

COMPOSITOR A person who composed type, that is, prepared the small blocks bearing words, numbers and symbols, for printing.

MASTER The first or main version of a recording, such as an audio disc or tape, or a movie, from which many copies are mass-produced.

OSCILLATOR An electrical device that makes a current oscillate, or reverse direction to and fro very quickly, which has the effect of sending out radio waves. It is a central part of a radio or television transmitter.

PRESS A machine (printing press) that prints newspapers, books and similar items. Also a general term for reporters, journalists, interviewers and other people gathering information for the media.

PRINT MEDIA News and information printed or otherwise put on to paper, as in books, magazines, journals, newspapers and posters.

RADIO The general name for the sound-only medium which uses invisible electromagnetic waves sent out, or broadcast, from transmitter to receiver. 'A radio' is also the everyday name for a radio receiver or radio set.

TELEGRAPHY 'Writing at a distance', a system of changing written words or other marks on paper into codes of electrical signals and sending them along wires or cables.

TELEPHONE 'Speaking at a distance', a system of changing spoken words or other sounds into codes of electrical signals and sending them along wires or cables.

VALVE An electronic device which looks like a small glass tube with metal parts (electrodes) inside. Valves have various jobs, such as using a very small, varying electric current to control a much larger current.

WIRELESS An early nickname for radio. Unlike the telegraph or telephone, the sender and receiver were not linked by wires, and so the system was said to be 'wire-less'. 'Wireless' also used to be the name for a radio receiver or radio set.

30

WORLD EVENTS

- Boxer Rising in China — 19
- Commonwealth of Australia proclaimed — 19
- Second Boer War ends in South Africa — 19
- UK 'Votes for Women' campaigns begin — 19
- Japan at war with Russia (to 1905) — 19
- First phase of Russian Revolution — 19
- San Francisco earthquake in USA — 19
- New Zealand acquires Dominion status — 19
- Austria annexes Bosnia-Herzegovina — 19
- Young Turks overthrow Sultan — 19
- Union of South Africa created — 19
- Chinese revolution: emperor overthrown — 19
- Balkan Wars (to 1913) — 19
- King George of Greece assassinated — 19
- Outbreak of World War I — 19
- ANZAC troops slaughtered on Gallipoli — 19
- Ireland: Easter Rising in Dublin — 19
- Russian Revolution
- USA enters war — 19
- World War I ends
- UK: women get vote — 19
- Treaty of Versailles
- Nazi Party founded — 19

TIMELINE

	HEADLINES	MEDIA EVENTS	MEDIA TECH	PERFORMANCE & ART
00	•Boer War: Siege of Mafeking relieved	•C. Arthur Pearson founds Daily Express newspaper	•Marconi Wireless Telegraphy Company	•Puccini: Tosca •Mahler: Fourth Symphony
01	•Queen Victoria of Great Britain dies	•New York Morning Journal becomes American	•Marconi sends radio signals across the Atlantic	•Chekhov: The Three Sisters
02	•Mt Pelée erupts	•The Times begins its Literary Supplement	•First mass-produced sound records (Caruso)	•A Trip to the Moon movie uses early special effects
03	•Wright brothers' first aeroplane flight	•UK's Daily Mirror founded	•First Western movie, using many location scenes	•Photo-Secession Camera Work journal begins
04	•New York: Subway opens at last	•W. R. Hearst attempts to become US president	•Photo-electric cell •Offset litho printing	•Joseph Conrad: Nostromo
05	•Einstein's Relativity: public baffled!	•Fauvist art causes a stir in Paris	•First nickelodeon film theatres, USA	•Strauss opera: Salome
06	•British Labour party founded	•'Muckraker' journalism rises to prominence	•Fessenden broadcasts voice and music by radio	•Schoenberg's First Chamber Symphony
07	•Ocean liner Lusitania makes first voyage	•United Press Association founded by E. W. Scripps	•Triode valve boosts radio and telegraph distances	•Picasso develops Cubism style of art
08	•Zeppelin airship disaster, Echterdingen	•Hearst tries to become governor of New York	•New Ford Model Ts used to deliver urgent reports	•Pathé-Journal newsreels begin
09	•Louis Blériot flies across the Channel	•Italy: Futurist movement publishes manifesto	•Radio pioneers Marconi & Braun share Nobel Prize	•Russian Ballet visits Paris
10	•Britain: George V becomes King	•Dr Crippen apprehended owing to radio	•London's The Times now set in Monotype	•Stravinsky: The Firebird
11	•Suffragette riots in UK	•Joseph Pulitzer dies	•Long-ish animated film Little Nemo	•Krazy Kat cartoon begins
12	•Ocean liner Titanic sinks, 1,500-plus drown	•The Times prints its last Christmas Day issue	•Daily Herald begins using newest print technology	•Keystone Kops movies begin
13	•India: Ghandi arrested	•Suffragette dies at Derby, reported in 100 countries	•Triode valves used for long-distance phone calls	•First International Exhibition of Modern Art
14	•Archduke Ferdinand assassinated, Sarajevo	•War brings powers of Press censorship	•IBM company founded	•Charlie Chaplin creates his 'Tramp' character
15	•Ocean liner Lusitania sunk by torpedo	•Chemical weapons first used in warfare	•First telephone call by radio across the Atlantic	•D. W. Griffiths movie The Birth of a Nation
16	•Battle of the Somme trench warfare	•Tanks first used in battle including Little Willie	•Goudy and Underground typefaces become popular	•Kafka: Metamorphosis
17	•Spy Mata Hari executed	•Dutch De Stijl avant-garde art magazine		•Mary Pickford stars in Poor Little Rich Girl
18	•Armistice signed	•UK: Northcliffe becomes Director of Propaganda	•First radio link between England and Australia	•Woolf: Night and Day
19	•Massacre at Amritsar, India; atom first split	•London-Paris daily air service carries reports		•Bauhaus design school founded in Germany

INDEX

American Civil War 23
Arbuckle, Fatty 23
Armstrong, Edwin 19
Atget, Eugène 27
autochrome 27

Bara, Theda 23
Baudot, Emile 14
Bell, Alexander 15
Bell Telephone 25
Berliner, Emile 24, 25
Bow, Clara 23
Braun, Karl 17
broadcasts 8, 16, 19
Bull, John 28

cables 14
cameras 20, 21 26, 29
cartoons 11, 12, 13, 28
Caruso, Enrico 25
cat's whisker 17
celluloid 21
Chaliapin, Fyodor 25
Chaplin, Charlie 23
children's matinées 23
cinema 5, 20, 21, 22, 23
Cinématographe 20, 21
Citizen Kane 11
Coburn, A. L. 26, 27
Colliers 12
colour photography 27
comic strips 13
compositors 8, 9
crime reporters 12
Crippen, Dr 18
crystal wireless set 17

Daily Mirror 11
De Forest, Lee 17
disasters 6, 7, 13
discs 24, 25

Edison, Thomas 20, 24
editors 10, 11
Edward VII, King 18
Elster, Johann 14
entertainment 5, 20, 25

fashion 11
Fessenden, R. 17, 19
films 20, 21, 22, 23
Fisher, Bud 13

gramophone 24, 25
Griffiths, D.W. 23

'hard' news 11
Harmsworth, Alfred 11
Hearst, W. R. 10, 11
Herriman, George 13
Hertz, Heinrich 16
Hines, Lewis 26, 27

illustrators 6
ink 8, 9
International Convention 7
investigative journalism 12

journalists 6, 11, 12, 15
journals 8

Kane, Charles Foster 11
Käsebier, Gertrude 27
Keystone Kops 22
Kinetoscope 20, 21
Kodak Brownie 26

layout 8
letterpress 8
Linotype 9
lithography 8
location 22
loudspeaker 17, 25
Lumière brothers 20, 27
Lusitania 29

McClure's 12
McCormack, John 25
McManus, George 13
magazines 5, 8, 11, 27
Marconi, Guglielmo 16, 17, 19
mass-production 26

Méliès, Georges 21
messengers 5, 8
microphones 25
Monotype 9
Montrose 18
Morse Code 6, 16, 18
Morse, Samuel 14
movies 5, 11, 21, 22–23
moving pictures 20–21
Muckrakers 12
multiplex 14
Muybridge, E. 20

New York Herald 29
New York Morning Journal 11
New York World 11
newspapers 4, 5, 7, 14, 18, 27, 28, 29
newspaper production 8–9
newspaper tycoons 10–11
newsreels 23
nickelodeons 23
Nobel Prize 17
Northcliffe, Lord 11

offset lithography 8–9

Pathé, Charles 23
periodicals 8
phonograph 24
photo-journalists 27
Photo-Secession 26, 27
photoelectric cell 14
photographs 5, 8, 13, 26–27
Pickford, Mary 23
Pope, the 25
Pound, Ezra 26
press barons 10–11
press services 11
printing 8–9
printing press 8, 9
projector 20
Pulitzer, Joseph 10, 11

radio 5, 6, 7, 8, 16–17, 18–19
radio stations 11
recorded sound 5, 24–25
records 25
reporters 7, 8, 12–13, 18
Roosevelt, President 12
Rubel, Ira W., 8
Russian Revolution 28

Scripps, Edward W. 11
Sennett, Mack 22
Sheffield Daily Telegraph 9
silent movies 22–23
sound recording 5, 24–25
special effects 21
Steichen, Edward 27
Stieglitz, Alfred 27
street vendors 8

telegrams 5, 14
telegraph 5, 8, 11, 14–15, 16
telephone 5, 11, 14, 15
television 5, 8
Titanic 6–7, 19
typesetting 9

United Press Association 11

Valentino, Rudolph 23
Victor Talking Machine Company 24

war 13, 19, 23, 28–29
Welles, Orson 11
White, Clarence 27
wireless 16–17, 19
wireless telegraphy 6
world news 13
Wright Brothers 14

yellow journalism 10
Yellow Kid, the 13